Apron Strings

Apron Strings

A Cookbook for Parents and Children

Lillian Gallego

authorHOUSE®

AuthorHouse™
1663 Liberty Drive
Bloomington, IN 47403
www.authorhouse.com
Phone: 1-800-839-8640

Published by AuthorHouse   01/10/2013

ISBN: 978-1-4772-4855-3 (sc)
ISBN: 978-1-4772-4854-6 (e)

Library of Congress Control Number: 2012912789

Contents

DESSERTS

For my husband Michael who
gave me the inspiration
to write this book

For my children Martin and Laurie
my first students
My daughter Sammi who
encouraged me to complete this book
For my granddaughter Evelyn
my newest student

For my sister Ronnie and my friend
Sally for their guidance and
support

Thank you
Mom and Mother Aunt Helen
for your support and encouragement
in developing my cooking skills.

Thank you
Dad
for eating all of my creations.

INTRODUCTION

One of my son and daughter's favorite activities was helping me in the kitchen. As an avid cook, I spent time teaching my children cooking and baking techniques. They helped prepare meals, baked treats and enjoyed eating what we created. Spending time in the kitchen with your children is fun and educational.

Safety always came first. I created a list of safety rules my children had to recite before we entered the kitchen. They knew that fire was hot, a knife was sharp and most important, **they were not allowed to be alone in the kitchen without an adult.**

Children can help in the kitchen at a young age, my children were just toddlers. They learned the colors and shapes of foods, as well as the differences between fruits and vegetables. I also designed simple structured activities to start; putting fruit on their French toast faces and bear pancakes, making fun shaped sandwiches, nutritious snacks, tossing a salad and making pudding.

Making your children's first attempt at cooking a successful and fun activity will give them a sense of accomplishment, confidence in themselves and pride in their creation. I have a vivid memory of my first attempt at cooking when I was five years old and visiting my grandmother. I was in the kitchen helping her prepare dinner and used some of the ingredients she was using to make her famous potato salad. I quickly mixed all the ingredients together in a small bowl and placed it on the dining room table. I insisted that my father try what I had created. He ate all of the potato salad and said it was the best he had ever tasted. Many years later he told me that the potato salad I made for him back then had raw potatoes in it. I didn't know that the potatoes had to be cooked. He did not want to hurt my feelings because he saw how proud I was of my accomplishment.

To get children started, design recipe cards using index cards. For younger children who are not yet able to read, draw symbols or use stickers for eggs, butter, fruit, pots and pans, bowls, spoons, etc. on the back of the index cards. This is a simple way for young children to follow a recipe. Laminating or using clear contact will protect the cards from being soiled or damaged. Wooden recipe boxes are great for storing recipe cards. Children can design their own recipe boxes using stickers or non-toxic markers. Keep recipe boxes in a special place in the kitchen within their reach.

Wearing an apron brings back such vivid memories. When I was a child, my grandmother embroidered my name on an apron that I used when I helped her in the kitchen. Wearing aprons in the kitchen gives children a sense of responsibility and maturity. My son and daughter enjoyed designing their own aprons. Children can show their creativity by designing their aprons using non-toxic fabric markers and fabric stickers. **Make sure that the apron fits well and that the apron strings are tied securely and tucked in the back to prevent accidents.** Keep the apron on a hook within their reach. All of these items can be purchased at a craft shop.

Cleaning is part of the cooking process. After the fun comes the clean up. My children did not always want to clean up the mess after cooking. I purchased a set of cooking utensils from our local store from which they each chose their own set of plastic mixing bowls, wooden spoons, plastic measuring cups, measuring spoons, spatulas, strainers, potholders and mitts, as well as bags to store their cooking utensils. I put these bags in a special place in the kitchen where they were accessible. I explained to them that these were their utensils for cooking and it was their responsibility to clean and take care of them. Both children took extra care cleaning and storing them. As their love for cooking grew they became even more diligent cleaning up after they cooked without me having to remind them.

Food shopping can be an educational and fun experience that children can enjoy when learning about cooking and baking. I've found that when you teach children while having fun, they seem to learn the task faster. When I went food shopping with my children, I gave them each a small list of needed items for the recipes we were making together. I made separate lists, one for each aisle and made sure that the items on the lists were within their reach. I designed lessons comparing sizes, weights and measures, frozen vs. canned, in addition to looking for the freshest fruits and vegetables.

This activity gave them the responsibility of choosing the correct items, which also kept them by my side while shopping in the store. They developed a better understanding of which ingredients were needed to complete the recipe.

My children assisted in making breakfast, lunch, snacks, dinner and desserts. They beat eggs, tossed salads, peeled potatoes and vegetables, mixed batter, made frosting, etc. They prepared, measured and mixed ingredients together. Each cooking activity included a lesson. They learned math by measuring liquid and dry ingredients. In addition, they learned the textures of sugar, brown sugar, baking powder and flour. They learned science by watching how yeast makes dough rise and is baked into bread. They learned sequencing by the order in which the ingredients were added. They acquired the specific techniques of sifting, mixing, stirring, blending and kneading, using a sieve, beating, whisks, spatulas and their hands respectively. One of their favorite activities was decorating cakes, pies and desserts. This involved preparing, filling and using a pastry bag, which included the use of different tips to make flowers, leaves and other designs.

As my children grew older, they learned more involved safety tips in the kitchen. This included using the back burners on the stove instead of the front burners and knowing to turn the pot handles in to prevent accidents, in addition to temperature control. They also learned the proper and safe way to use a knife. As time went on, they challenged themselves to try more difficult recipes that involved different techniques.

The fun part comes when you and your children are able to sit down and enjoy eating what you created together. When we were sitting down to eat, I would always mention to my family how the children helped me make the meal. Of course, everyone clapped and said how good the food tasted and what a good job they did. We saw the pride in their eyes, the happiness in their smiles, and the success they felt in what they helped create.

As children develop their cooking skills and learn more, encourage them to use their imagination when preparing meals or decorating cakes. Inspire them to create their own recipes. Motivate them to keep a journal and write down their recipes or enter them onto a computer. Also let them know that cooking is trial and error. All cooks, even famous ones, have had some failures, but that's how we learn from our mistakes. Encourage them to continue trying. Also, research recipes passed down from your family. Many families have passed down recipes from their ancestors.

To form the face: use 1 banana slice for each eye, top each banana slice with 1 blueberry. Use 1 blueberry for the nose and 1 apple, pear or peach crescent for the mouth. Repeat with remaining French toast rounds. Serve immediately. Other fruits can be substituted according to taste.

Makes 4 servings.

* **Tip:** *Butter the spatula for easy turning and lifting out of the pan.*

FRUITY BEAR PANCAKES

This is another breakfast favorite with no syrup needed.

Pancake batter from prepared mix for 8 large pancakes
Butter, margarine or cooking spray to grease pan and cookie cutters
Bananas thinly sliced
Blueberries
Apples, pears or peaches cut into thinly sliced crescents

Use one large round cookie cutter for the bear's body, one medium round cookie cutter for the bear's head and two small round cookie cutters for the ears. Lightly grease the inside of the cookie cutters. Prepare fruit for faces and set aside.

Lightly grease a large frying pan. Arrange the cookie cutters on the prepared pan so that all the sides are touching. Heat the pan to medium heat. Pour the prepared pancake batter into the center of each of the cookie cutters filling them completely about half way up the sides. The pancake will rise as it cooks. After about 2 minutes or when the pancake is set, gently remove the cookie cutters. With a large buttered spatula, gently flip the pancake over to cook the other side about 1 minute or until lightly browned. Remove the pancake from the pan and keep warm. Repeat with the remaining pancake batter.

Place the bear pancakes on serving plates. To form the face: use 1 banana slice for each eye, top each banana slice with 1 blueberry. Use 1 blueberry for the nose and 1 apple, pear or peach crescent for the mouth. Repeat with remaining bear pancakes. Serve immediately. Other fruits can be substituted according to taste.

Makes 4 servings.

* **Tip:** *Butter the spatula for easy turning and lifting out of the pan.*

HAPPY FACE EGGS
IN A BREAD FRAME

2   Slices white or wheat bread
    Butter, margarine or cooking spray to grease pan
4   Medium size eggs
    Bacon, sliced sausage, ham or cheese for the nose and mouth

Use a large round cookie cutter or wide-mouth glass to cut out the center of each bread slice. Discard the center.

Lightly grease a large frying pan. Heat the pan to medium heat. Place one bread frame at a time in the middle of the frying pan.

Crack two eggs into the center of the bread frame to make the eyes. With a buttered spatula, gently move the yokes of the eggs to the top of the bread frame. Add the bacon, sausage, ham or cheese to complete the face. Cook about 1 minute or until the bottom is set. With a large buttered spatula, gently flip the bread frame over. Continue to cook 1 minute for loose yokes or 2 minutes for stiff yokes. Flip it over again to show the face. Remove the bread frame from the pan and keep warm. Repeat with the remaining bread slice. Serve immediately.

Makes 2 serving.

* **Tip**: *Butter the spatula for easy turning and lifting out of the pan.*

LUNCH

FUN FOOD CUT OUT SANDWICHES

My children loved making and eating cut out snacks and sandwiches.

Trying to get your children to eat nutritious foods that are good for them is not always easy. I found a fun and easy way to get my children to eat healthy snacks such as cheese, fruits, etc. Purchase a collection of cookie cutters in fun sizes and shapes that you know your children will like. Cookie cutters can be found in your local craft shops.

Use any sliced cheese, American, Munster, Swiss, etc. and using the cookie cutters make fun shapes for your child for lunch or just for a snack.

When using a large shaped cookie cutter, such as animals, cars, flowers, trees, boats, etc., your child can make fun shaped sandwiches to eat. Make your child's favorite sandwich, peanut butter and jelly, ham and cheese, tuna fish, egg salad, etc. Then have your child cut out the center of the bread using the cookie cutter.

Another idea for your children's lunch is making fun face sandwiches. With a large round cookie cutter, cut out the center of any sandwich bread. Use any sandwich spread such as, cream cheese, peanut butter and jelly or whatever your children enjoy. Cover the entire bread round with the spread and then they can decorate the round using raisins, dried cranberries and other dried fruits for the eyes, nose and mouth. Your children will have fun making and eating their creations. Rice cakes can also be used instead of bread.

MINI PIZZAS

My children's favorite meal, fun to make and eat.

    Butter, margarine or cooking spray to grease pan
1 **Tube 7.5 ounces round refrigerated biscuits**
1 **Cup spaghetti sauce**
2 **Cups shredded mozzarella cheese**
    Optional toppings—pepperoni, sausage, mushrooms, etc.

Preheat oven to 450 degrees. Grease a cookie sheet with butter, margarine or cooking spray.

Remove biscuits from the tube. Place one biscuit at a time on the cookie sheet. Using two fingers press the middle of the biscuit down working around the entire center, leaving the edges intact as a crust. Continue with the rest of the biscuits, leaving 1 inch of space between each one.

Spoon sauce onto the middle of each biscuit. Top with shredded mozzarella cheese. Add optional toppings if desired.

Bake 10 minutes at 450 degrees or until lightly brown. With a spatula carefully remove the mini pizzas and place on a platter. Serve immediately.

Makes 10 pizzas.

PASTA SALAD

1   Box 16 ounces bow tie pasta
1   Small red onion sliced
3   Celery ribs sliced
1   Red pepper cubed
3   Carrot sticks sliced
1   Head broccoli tops broken up
1   Jar 6 ounces marinated artichoke hearts (drained) cut in half
1½ Cups mayonnaise
¼   Cup white distilled vinegar

Cook pasta according to package directions, drain and cool. Meanwhile prepare vegetables.

Combine cooled pasta with vegetables. Mix mayonnaise and vinegar. Add to pasta and vegetable mixture. Gently toss to coat completely. Serve cold.

Makes 6 to 8 servings.

PINWHEEL SANDWICHES

A fun lunchtime treat or after school snack.
Great for sleepovers.

- **4 Slices white bread**
- **4 Ounces whipped cream cheese softened**
- **1 Cup chopped raisins or dried cranberries**

Cut the crust off each slice of bread. Place one slice of bread between two pieces of wax paper. With a rolling pin, roll over the bread to flatten. Remove the wax paper and set the flattened bread aside. Repeat with the remaining bread slices.

Combine the cream cheese and raisins or cranberries. Spread the cream cheese mixture over each flattened bread slice. Roll the bread into a jellyroll. Cover with wax paper tightly and twist edges to seal. If necessary secure with tape. Refrigerate 2 to 3 hours.

When set, unwrap the rolls and with a sharp knife, cut each into bite size pieces. Serve with fruit.

Makes approximately16 pieces.

Other Spreads: *Peanut Butter,*
Tuna Salad & egg Salad.

SNACKS

SNACKS

FROZEN BANANAS DIPPED IN CHOCOLATE

This was the only way my daughter would eat bananas.

- 4 **Bananas (ripe but not over ripe)**
- 8 **Craft sticks (Popsicle sticks)**
- 1 **Bag 11.5 ounces semi-sweet chocolate chips**
  Chopped nuts optional

Cut bananas in half. Put one craft stick into the middle cut end of each banana half and peel off the skin. Wrap the bananas in plastic wrap and freeze 4 to 5 hours or overnight.

Melt the chocolate chips in a double boiler or in a microwave oven. Pour the melted chocolate into a tall wide heat resistant glass. Prepare a cookie sheet lined with wax paper.

Unwrap the bananas and hold each one by the craft stick, dip the entire banana into the melted chocolate and coat completely. Immediately roll the chocolate covered bananas in the chopped nuts if desired. Place the bananas onto the wax-papered cookie sheet and put back into the freezer until fully frozen.

Makes 8 bananas.

FROZEN PUDDING POPS

A cool and refreshing dessert on a hot day.

1   Box 3.8 ounces instant chocolate or vanilla pudding and pie filling
2   Cups whole milk
6   Craft sticks (Popsicle sticks) optional

Make pudding according to the package directions. Spoon the pudding into six freezer cups with attached sticks used to make frozen desserts or spoon into six small paper cups and insert a craft stick into each cup. Freeze until set.

To remove the pudding pops, twist the freezer cups and the pops should slip out. If necessary, dip the cups into warm water 1 or 3 seconds to remove the pops.

Makes 6 pops.

FUN FRUIT TREATS

Fruit Cutouts on a Stick

> **Cantaloupe**
> **Honeydew**
> **Watermelon**
> **Pineapple**
> **Small cookie cutters**
> **Craft sticks (Popsicle sticks)**

Cut fruit into 1 inch slices. Place the cookie cutter in the middle of each fruit slice and cut into shape. Insert a craft stick into the bottom of each shape. Also try putting these fruit shapes in the freezer for a cool frozen treat.

Frozen Fruit Pops

This was my way of getting the swelling down when my child had a fat lip.

> **Cantaloupe**
> **Pineapple**
> **Apples**
> **Honeydew**
> **Peaches**
> **Oranges**
> **Grapefruit**
> **Mango**

Cut fruit into small pieces and put into a blender or food processor. Use the pulse setting, crush the fruit just until it is mushy, don't over crush.

Spoon the fruit into freezer cups with attached sticks used to make frozen desserts or spoon into small paper cups and insert a craft stick into each cup. Freeze until set.

To remove the fruit pops, twist the freezer cups and the pops should slip out. If necessary, dip the cups into warm water 1 to 3 seconds to remove pops.

DINNER

CHEESY CHICKEN SANDWICHES

1   Cup all purpose flour
¼   Teaspoon salt
1   Teaspoon garlic powder
½   Teaspoon basil
¼   Cup grated parmesan cheese
4   Thinly sliced chicken cutlets
1   Tablespoon cooking oil
    Medium sandwich rolls

Combine flour, salt, garlic powder, basil and parmesan cheese in a large unused plastic bag, for drenching chicken. Set aside.

Wash and completely dry chicken cutlets with paper towels. Place one chicken cutlet at a time into the prepared plastic bag. Shake the bag to completely cover chicken with the flour mixture. Repeat with the remaining cutlets.

Heat the cooking oil in a large frying pan on medium heat. Add the chicken cutlets and cook for 3 to 4 minutes. Turn and cook for 2 minutes longer or until chicken is white inside.

Drain cutlets thoroughly on paper towels. Slice rolls and place one cutlet on each roll. Serve with a salad.

Makes 4 servings.

DEEP DISH TURKEY POT PIE

Not only is this a fast 1-dish meal, your children can use their imagination when decorating with dough.

1   **Package 1 to 1 ½ pounds turkey cutlets**
1   **Can 15 ounces sliced potatoes drained**
1   **Package 16 ounces frozen mixed vegetables**
1   **Jar 12 ounces turkey gravy**
1   **Tube 8 ounces refrigerator crescent rolls**

Preheat oven to 375 degrees.

Cut the turkey cutlets into bite size pieces. In a large pot cook turkey on low heat covered for 3 minutes or until white in color. Add the drained potatoes, frozen mixed vegetables, and turkey gravy. Mix well. Cook for 7 minutes covered on low heat stirring occasionally.

Pour turkey mixture evenly into an 8x8 inch-baking dish. Open the crescent rolls. Unroll each roll onto a cutting board. Pinch perforations closed in order to make it into one piece of dough. Cut dough in order to fit over the turkey mixture. Decorate with the remaining dough. Bake at 375 degrees for 11-13 minutes or until lightly browned. Serve hot.

Makes 2 to 4 servings.

Chicken or Beef can be substituted

HAWAIIAN HAM

1   Fully cooked ham steak 1 to 1½ pounds
2   Tablespoons soy sauce
1   Can 20 ounces pineapple chunks in juice
1   Large red pepper cut into chunks
½   Cup dark packed brown sugar
1   Teaspoon cornstarch
½   Cup water
    Cooked rice

Cut the ham steak into chunks. In a large pot, add ham and cook on medium heat. Add the soy sauce, pineapple chunks and juice and the red pepper.

Cook until fully heated, about 5 to 7 minutes. Reduce the heat to low and add the brown sugar, stir until fully combined. Mix the cornstarch and water together until the cornstarch is completely dissolved. Add to the ham mixture to thicken.

Serve with rice.

Makes 2 to 4 servings.

Turkey or Chicken cutlets can replace ham

NOODLE DELIGHT

1   Package 12 ounces broad egg noodles
½   Pound cooked sliced ham
½   Pound sliced pepperoni
8   Ounces shredded mozzarella cheese
    Parmesan cheese
    Cooked broccoli, carrots, cauliflower optional

Cook noodles according to package directions. Meanwhile cut ham into bite size pieces, cut pepperoni slices in half.

When noodles are fully cooked, drain well and place in a large serving bowl. Add ham, pepperoni and mozzarella cheese, and mix until complete combined. Add vegetables if desired.

Before serving sprinkle with Parmesan cheese. Serve with hot rolls.

Makes 3 to 4 servings.

SURPRISE HAMBURGERS

The fun is being surprised.

2   **Pounds lean ground beef**
½   **Cup flavored breadcrumbs**
4   **Hamburger buns**

Fillings

Raw onion
Fried onions
Chopped ham and cheese
Sautéed mushrooms
Cooked crumpled bacon
Chopped red and green peppers

Preheat oven to 350 degrees. Mix the breadcrumbs into the ground beef. Shape into eight thin patties.

Place 1 tablespoon of the fillings onto one patty. Top with another patty and seal the edges around the entire patty.

Place the patties into a baking pan and bake at 350 degrees for 20 to 25 minutes or until completely cooked. Carefully remove the surprise hamburgers and place them on the buns.

Makes 4 servings

DESSERTS

APPLE ROLL

My children love apple pie and this is a quick and easy apple dessert that takes a short time to make.

2   **Red delicious apples**
1   **Tablespoon butter or margarine**
2   **Tablespoons sugar**
1   **Teaspoon cinnamon**
    Butter, margarine or cooking spray to grease pan
1   **Tube 7.5 ounces round refrigerated biscuits**
    Powdered sugar to dust

Preheat oven to 450 degrees. Peel and core apples, slice thinly. Heat butter or margarine in a frying pan over medium heat. Add the apples and coat. Reduce heat to low, add the sugar and cinnamon. Mix gently so not to break the apples. Cook for two minutes. Set aside.

Grease the middle length of a medium size cookie sheet with butter or margarine. Open the tube of biscuits. Take out two biscuits at a time laying them side-by-side on the greased upper part of the cookie sheet. With your fingers, gently press the biscuits a bit to stretch them out so they are touching. Pinch the two touching ends together. Continue working with the rest of the biscuits, pressing them and pinching them together working down the length of the cookie sheet until you have one solid rectangle of dough.

Holding the outer part of the dough and using two fingers, (thumb and pointer to hold the dough in place) take a sharp knife and make little slits between your two fingers down each side of the length of the rectangle of dough leaving the middle of the dough intact.

Spoon the apple mixture down the middle length of the dough. Starting from the top and working down to the end, pull one piece of dough over the apples to the other side of the dough. Then alternate pulling each piece of dough over the apples to the other side, leaving some of the apples showing. It should look like the dough is braided over the apples. Gently press down on the dough to seal.

Bake at 450 degrees for 10 minutes or until lightly browned. With a spatula carefully transfer the apple roll to a cutting board and cut into slices. Dust with powdered sugar. Serve immediately.

Makes 4 servings.

Peaches or Pears can be substituted

BLUEBERRY BOTTOM PUDDING PIE

1   Box 3.8 ounces instant vanilla pudding and pie filling
1   Cup whole milk
1   Container 8 ounces frozen whipped topping thawed
1   9 inch graham cracker piecrust
1½ Cups fresh blueberries
    Prepared white frosting for decorating

Pour pudding and pie filling into a large mixing bowl. Add milk. Mix well until completely combined. Pudding will be thick.

Add half of the whipped topping to pudding and mix well until complete combined. Set aside.

Wash and drain blueberries in a colander, make sure they are dry (use paper towels). Arrange 1 cup of the blueberries into the bottom of the piecrust, reserve ½ cup for decorating.

Spoon the pudding mixture over the blueberries and spread evenly. Cover the pudding mixture completely with the remaining whipped topping.

Use a 12-inch pastry bag fitted with a star tip, pipe frosting around the edges of the piecrust. Decorate with remaining blueberries. Refrigerate 3 hours.

Makes 6 to 8 servings.

See the tip on Graham Cracker Holiday Houses for filling a pastry bag

BROWNIE POPS

These brownie pops sold out at the PTA cake sales.

2   Eggs
¾   Cup sugar
1   Teaspoon vanilla
¼   Cup (½ stick) unsalted butter melted
¼   Cup cocoa (sifted)
1   Cup flour
1   Teaspoon baking powder
6   to 8 craft sticks (Popsicle sticks)
    Prepared frosting for decorating
    Sprinkles, candy, etc. for decorating

Preheat oven to 350 degrees. Lightly grease an 8x8-inch square-baking pan.

Beat the eggs well in a large mixing bowl. Add the sugar and mix until fully combined. Pour in the vanilla and melted butter and continue to mix until completely incorporated.

Add the sifted cocoa and mix until fully combined. Sift the flour and baking powder together. Add to the cocoa mixture, mix just until combined. Do not over mix.

Spread the batter evenly into the prepared pan. Bake at 350 degrees for 35 to 45 minutes. Let cool completely.

To unmold the brownie, run a dull knife around the edges to loosen the brownie. Cover a cutting board with wax paper to prevent sticking. Place the cutting board over the pan and invert. If the brownie does not come out run the knife around again. Use a sharp knife to cut the brownie into small pop size shapes. Insert one craft stick into the flat bottom of each brownie pop. Spread the top and sides of each brownie pop with frosting and place on a cookie sheet lined with wax paper.

Decorate as desired.

Makes 6 to 8 pops.

CHOCOLATE PUDDING PIE

This is a quick and easy no bake dessert.

1   Box 3.8 ounces instant chocolate pudding and pie filling
2   Cups whole milk
1   Container 8 ounces frozen whipped topping thawed
1   9-inch graham cracker piecrust
    Chocolate chips, sprinkles, etc. for decorating
    Prepared white frosting for decorating

Mix the pudding and pie filling with milk in a large mixing bowl. Mix well until completely combined.

Spoon the pudding into the piecrust and spread evenly. Cover the pudding mixture completely with the whipped topping. Decorate using chocolate chips, sprinkles, etc.

Use a 12-inch pastry bag fitted with a star tip, pipe the frosting around the edges of the piecrust. Refrigerate 3 hours.

Makes 6 to 8 servings.

See the tip on Graham Cracker Holiday Houses for filling a pastry bag

EASY MINI STRAWBERRY SHORTCAKES

This was one of the first desserts I made with my children.

1   **Package 6 cake cups—5 ounces**
1   **Pint fresh strawberries**
1   **Container 8 ounces frozen whipped topping thawed**

Each mini strawberry short cake will require two cake cups.

Cut off the rim from three of the cake cups. Remove the stems from six strawberries and thinly slice lengthwise.

To assemble the cake, spread 2 tablespoons of the whipped topping into the cake cup. Layer the sliced strawberries over the topping. Spread 1 tablespoon whipped topping over the strawberries. Cover with the cake cup with the removed rim cut side down. Spread 2 tablespoons of the whipped topping over the top of the cake.

For decorating, thinly slice the middle of a strawberry lengthwise leaving the top and stem intact. Using one or two fingers, gently push the strawberry slices down in order to spread them into a fan for decoration. Place fanned strawberry over topping. Cool in refrigerator until ready to serve.

Makes 3 servings.

GRAHAM CRACKER HOLIDAY HOUSES

This fun activity was a favorite at our house around the holidays.

- 1   Box 14.4 ounces graham crackers containing 3 packs each
- 3   Containers 16 ounces prepared white frosting
- 3   Cardboard rounds (6 inches in diameter)
- 2   Bags 11.5 ounces chocolate chips
- 3   Bags10 ounce gum drops
- 2   Bags10.5 ounces mini marshmallows
     Small candy canes

Each pack of graham crackers makes 1 house.

Put chocolate chips, gum drops, mini marshmallow, small candy canes and any other decoration into separate bowls for easy access when decorating the holiday houses.

Carefully open each pack of graham crackers keeping them intact. Place on a large plate to keep them from breaking.

Spread a thick layer of frosting onto the cardboard round spreading evenly and covering the entire round. Gently place the crackers onto the frosted round using frosting to hold the ends together. Continue to build the graham cracker house securing it with additional frosting.

When the house is complete, use a 12-inch pastry bag fitted with a star tip to pipe the frosting around the seams of the house. Decorate with chocolate chips, gum drops, marshmallows and candy canes. Raisins, dried cranberries or nuts can also be used. Store the finished houses in a cool dry place.

Makes 3 houses.

* **Tip:** *When filling a pastry bag, cut the tip of the pastry bag so that the coupling will fit in securely. Put the coupling inside the pastry bag using your second finger (pointer); the coupling should fit in tight. Insert the decorative tip over the bag and coupling; making sure that it covers the entire end. Put the coupling band over the bag and tip and twist it until it's tight and the tip is straight and secure.*

Hold the pastry bag in one hand and fold the bag over your entire hand so that there is a wide area to fill. Using a spoon or spatula, fill the pastry bag (at least half full) with frosting then close your hand over the spoon or spatula allowing the frosting to stay in the bag. Gently remove the spoon or spatula keeping your hand closed. Repeat as necessary.

Twist the top of the bag closed to avoid the frosting from coming out through the top. Hold the top of the bag tightly so not to untwist. Using your other hand, carefully push the frosting from the top of the bag down towards the tip. Continue working your way down pushing the frosting through the tip. You will have to twist the bag tighter as the frosting goes down. Refill bag as needed.

Printed in the United States
By Bookmasters